GROWING OUTSIDE THE WOMB

(A NICU Miracle)

GIOVANNI CALLUM PATTERSON

Copyright © 2020 by Candace Fox and Calvin Patterson . 820401

All rights reserved. No part of this book may be reproduced
or transmitted in any form or by any means, electronic or
mechanical, including photocopying, recording, or by any
information storage and retrieval system, without permission in
writing from the copyright owner.

To order additional copies of this book, contact:
Xlibris
844-714-8691
www.Xlibris.com
Orders@Xlibris.com

ISBN: Softcover   978-1-6641-3474-4
         EBook   978-1-6641-3473-7

Print information available on the last page

Rev. date: 10/09/2020

Acknowledgement

I would like to first give the thanks to God for working through the mind of man to nurse our son Giovanni back to health.

Women's Hospital

Thomas Saltau, MD Neonatologist

Kimberly Stewart, MD Neonatologist

We thank you and all nurses for your support! You guys were there every step of the way, and your kindness will never be forgotten.

Family and friends we appreciate you and love you very much!

May blessings be upon you all.

Introduction

As you do not know the path of the wind or how the body is formed in a mother's womb so you cannot understand the work of God, the maker of all things. Ecclesiastes 11:5 NIV

Code Blue! Code Blue! The sound of doctors and nurses pierced my ears rushing me to the nearest delivery room. As they are rolling me I can feel my child coming half way out! This was one of the scariest feelings in the world it felt like a pack of slime gushing out of me literally. The pain, sweat, tears you begin to ask yourself is it all worth it? Two minutes had passed and we heard the small cry of a sweet baby boy born at twenty-three weeks on June 2, 2018 at 10:15 a.m. weighing 1lb. 3o.z., 11.8 in. we decided to name him Giovanni Callum Patterson. When our baby was born we were told that Giovanni only had a thirty percent chance of survival but we believed in God only. I'm pretty sure there were many babies whose parents were told the same thing but God always have other plans different than our own. We can't question the work of God and no one will ever know how NICU parents feel that's why we are here to share our journey with all that's experiencing the same or similar situations. It doesn't matter if you have a NICU experience or not you yourself may have an underlying condition but always remember God is in control not man.

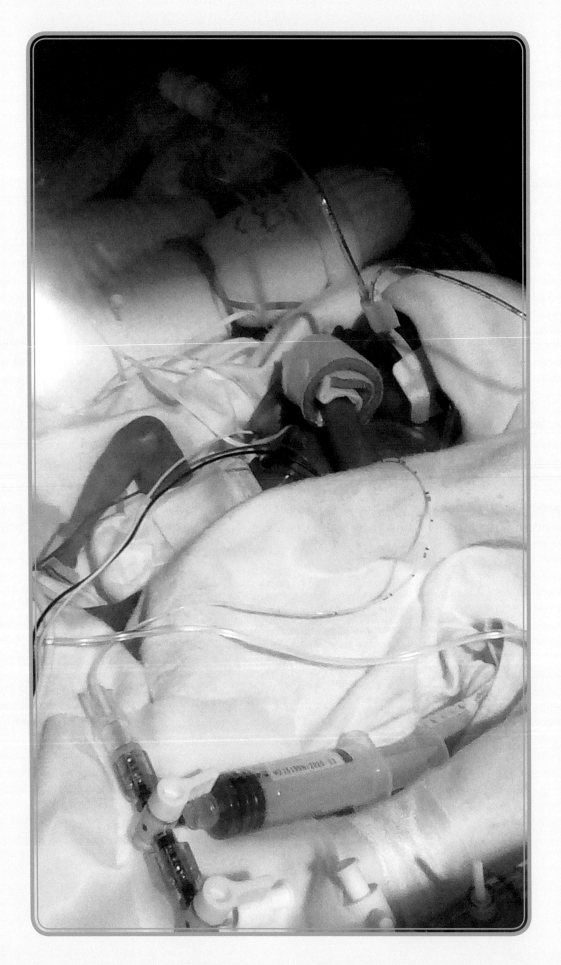

1
C H A P T E R

Differentiated Changes

Children are a gift from God; they are his reward. Psalm 127:3 NIV

The NICU (Neonatal Intensive Care Unit) is an intensive care nursery where babies are born prematurely, problems occurring during delivery, and if there are signs of a health condition that needs monitoring they will be sent there. However, Giovanni was considered a "micro preemie" which is a baby born weighing less than eight hundred grams so you do the math. According to statistics fifty percent to sixty-six percent of babies survive at twenty-three weeks.

When Giovanni was admitted to the NICU the staff was pretty welcoming. To the staff all the "micro preemies" are very different versus a baby that was born full term with minor issues. The "micro preemies" are born way too early but look on the bright side as parents you get to watch your baby grow outside the womb! We were confused why our baby looked so different like an alien rather but seeing your baby physically growing outside the womb gives you hope everyday. I had to learn to appreciate this experience eventually and so will you if this situation happens.

The staff at the NICU works extremely hard to ensure that all babies who are born early stay warm in isolettes. We couldn't quite figure it out why Giovanni had gel like skin in his first week of being in there but we had to remember they are mimicking how he was in my womb. Some people may not understand how this feels because they never been through it which is understandable. Our child was hooked up to all kind of I've and a breathing machine that was doing the majority of the work for him. As a mom you have a different kind of bond with your child and to go through this with my first child was very heart breaking. I wish I could have taken his place in that hospital for months but God gave him life to have a testimony. After about a week the doctor called us and said Giovanni had an open blood vessel around his heart. I will share this with you guys the power of God through fasting and praying when your baptized in Jesus name you will get relief. In two days the hole was closed and it never reopened isn't that powerful. To all parents God can do anything for your child just trust him.

2
CHAPTER

Self-Blame Mom

Beloved don't be surprised at the fiery ordeal when it comes upon to test you, as
though something strange were happening to you. 1 Peter 4:12 AMP

As a mom when you have a baby in the NICU you feel as though you are helpless and you have
failed your baby as a mom to start. When Giovanni first went got admitted the lactation nurse
came and introduced pumping to me. They provided organic tea called "Mom's Milk" that tasted
like licorice jelly beans. Have you ever received jelly beans for a holiday and notice everyone eat all
the good flavors except for the nasty licorice one? Well that just wasn't working out for me but who
says it won't for you. Although, I attempted to pump for two weeks even eating lactation cookies
I still was only able to provide a little milk. However, after trying all those methods pumping
became so stressful being I was unsuccessful I stopped. This hurt me to my heart because as a
mom I felt like I lacked the one thing Giovanni needed the most his own mother's milk. When
the nurse gave me the option to get donor milk I went with it because anything is better than
processed formula. I'm a true supporter of organic unprocessed everything so I was grateful to hear
there was a donor to provide Giovanni's milk. With this being said my advice to NICU moms of
miracles if you can't pump milk and you've exhausted all of your options accept the donors milk.
As a mom or dad when you see your micro preemie with feeding tubes, iv lines, arterial lines,
monitors and hooked up to a ventilator a heavy burden is weighed on your heart. Their skin is
very thin, with veins you can see and their skin resembles a gel-like substance slime for example,
After witnessing all of these things we didn't know that's where the self-blame comes in.

You begin to ask the question if I would have done things in the pregnancy different could this have
been avoided? Well the answer is no because God ways are not our ways. It's not by accident that
you become a mom of a micro preemie baby it actually is what God has for you. I wouldn't dare
question my father but it made me wonder why such thing would occur with my first born child.
Sometimes we may ask God for things but he doesn't ever make a promise to give it to us perfect.

I was explaining to my fiancé what a friend in West Virginia passed down to me which was "If
God didn't think you guys were up for the NICU challenge he wouldn't have choose you guys
as parents of one" . She herself was also the mom of a twenty three week miracle which gave
us more hope knowing that God is everywhere. It made me feel a little at ease to know that

another mom felt my pain. So to all the NICU miracle moms don't blame yourself because your baby needs positivity, prayers, and strength. There is no room for doubt, self-blame and the lack of faith. Just look at the bright side you actually have front row seats to watch your baby do everything he/she was doing inside of the womb! It honestly doesn't get no interesting than that. This is by far the most intense experience we have ever encountered so sudden. Always say I don't know what your doing God but I know it's wonderful. The purpose you have on our child life is unknown but by your grace we will ensure it's fulfilled in your will. You may have to go through some things in life but always remember there is a rainbow on the other side.

3
CHAPTER

Adapting to the NICU

It was a little unsettling knowing that we were in June and the NICU would be our temporary home until September. As a mom even a dad it's pretty heart breaking and stressful at times no matter how much you pray. It makes you think how they have moms that smoke, drink and do things that are unacceptable in the pregnancy the entire nine months yet they still deliver babies full term. Then you have a mom like myself that eats healthy as a vegetarian consuming organic products only taking expensive raw prenatal but still deliver a twenty three week baby. I know your probably wondering as well but God issued this temporary home. We as parents have to learn to pray and adapt to God's will so our babies can go home with us at the right time.

However, it's a blessing that God works through the mind of man to get NICU miracles right where they need to be. It's not easy adapting to the NICU because there is always monitors going off. Our sweet boy was on the side with the micro preemies and they don't scream being that their lungs are premature or undeveloped rather. There are certain things we had to adapt to in the NICU such as turning the light on before touching your baby in the incubator, continuously sanitizing our hands and not being able to show physical affection to him only through hand hugs. A hand hug is when you take your hand and cups their little bodies letting them feel your warm love. At first I was afraid to do hand hugs because the texture of my baby skin. After a while it became the new normal for us and I enjoyed the connection that was being established between Giovanni and us.

Although hand hugs are great but it can become difficult for parents because it's your baby you should be able to do as you please. I was one of those parents that questioned nurses and doctors about everything concerning Giovanni. It took some time they understood sympathizing with us being that it was a new yet long process. My advice to you from experience is to follow the protocol of the NICU because it's for the safety of parents & babies.

My biggest issue was Giovanni being naked all the time with a diaper on and I wanted him in clothes badly. Everyday I would bring clothes and ask the nurse can he wear clothing yet? She would say not quite yet but we are almost there and my heart would get crushed all over again. She went on to explaining when your child is that small the doctors and nurses need to be able to get to them quickly in case of an emergency. That's why they have to wait a certain amount of weeks to put clothes on them which I understand that now. The nurse showed us compassion and she explained that the NICU wants the same for you and your child just please be patient with them doing their job. That bought a great relief to my heart and it encouraged me to order more micro preemie clothes trusting God one day Giovanni will be wearing them.

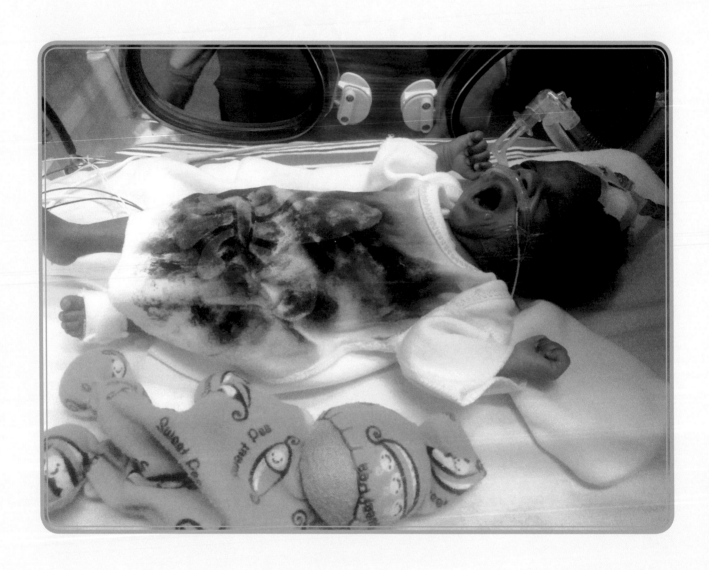

4
CHAPTER

Growth and Progress

"Nevertheless the righteous will hold to his way, and he who has clean
hands will grow stronger and stronger. Job 17:9 AMP

Giovanni weighed almost five pounds at the end of August and the staff was astonished by his progress. When God is in the process what can possibly go wrong especially if you're a believer. Our child was born at twenty-three weeks and it's amazing to see how much progress he has shown over the past months. In all honesty the only battle we faced was oxygen he was requiring more some days and breathing on his own very little. Let me tell you we continued to keep praying all week and when we went in his room to check on him the nurse said he is only requiring one percent of oxygen. That was like music to our ears because we were moving at a steady pace and didn't need any setbacks. What a testimony! God will never leave you all you have to do is put your trust in him with every situation. Some people may consider it as lucky but we say we are blessed by God's grace. When you're a parent (especially a new one like myself) this can be a very stressful process because we are still in the flesh. Even though the hospital visits wasn't always pleasant we made it through. If you are the parents of a NICU miracle and your reading this remember the word endurance! Things will get better just trust and believe in God throughout the process. It's not always who start the race but it's the one that makes it to the finish line. Your baby situation may be similar or different from ours but you guys will be fine. Even if you don't have a similar experience but you may have underlying health conditions prayer changes everything. I'm here to encourage you because I know how it feels to be at rock bottom. It feels as though you are climbing to the top then you slip back to the bottom. All we can do as parents of any child is to pray for them continuously believing that better days lie ahead. Faith without works is dead! However, when you can consistently be there and continue to care for your child in the hospital it's a blessing. This experience has made a lasting impact on both our lives. We wrote this book for Giovanni because this is his testimony. I don't ever want him to forget where God has taken him from.

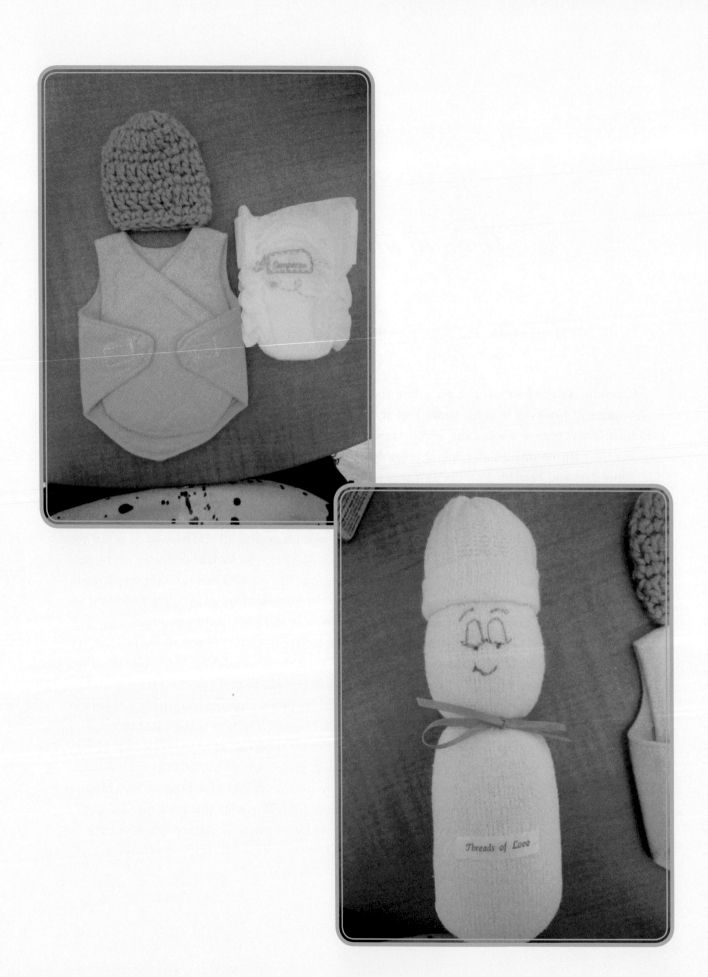

CHAPTER

NICU Departure

Rejoice in the Lord always: and again I say Rejoice. Let your moderation be
known to all men. The Lord is at hand. Philippians 4:4-5 KJV

I would never forget on September 14, 2018 we received the phone call of a lifetime. The doctor told us that our Giovanni was ready to come home. That was good news to us but of course it came with stipulations. He said in order for Giovanni to come home you have to come in to let the nurse train you on the oxygen equipment. I was thinking that since Giovanni's due date wasn't until September 29, 2018 that they would keep him as they instructed until that date. When you trust God miraculous things take place and we will never be able to figure his ways out. When the doctor said that my heart felt like is was a ship floating good until it sunk. We didn't know how to care for a child on oxygen that's a hurtful feeling because you can't even show affection properly. Put yourself in our shoes we had been seeing him on machines since birth and to hear one has to come home with us was disturbing. I was a little scared because I didn't believe I would remember all the equipment. At that point your thinking all kind of thoughts like what I'm going to do the hospital is no longer involved. I didn't want anything to go wrong and my child end up back at square one. However, as the lady nurse was showing us the equipment chills was running down my spine. My fiancé was all into it and he immediately learned how to use the equipment. Seeing him do it made me a little bit more comfortable because I was angry inside not accepting this change. We were given a monitor, portable oxygen (used for dr. appointments, outings, etc.) and a back up oxygen tank that's to last for seventy-two hours in case of emergency. I couldn't be upset with the doctors and nurses being they worked hard nursing our baby boy to health. Without God working through the mind of man we wouldn't have even made it this far. Giovanni was sent home on thyroid medicine and one percent of oxygen. The doctor who has been in practice for twenty-six years told us Giovanni was the first baby he ever released before their due date. As previously mentioned Giovanni's due date was September 29, 2018 but God plans were much different and I delivered him on June 2, 2018. To my knowledge from the doctor a baby that's born at twenty-three weeks can't leave the hospital until their due date or after. I may have been upset crying over the oxygen but our baby boy needed zero surgeries. I was also told if a baby is showing they know how to eat (tolerate feeds) has a nice suck pattern (with their bottle) and they are able to continue growing without fluctuation they may go home.

We encountered other parents that had babies born at thirty-four weeks who still couldn't go home and they were more developed than Giovanni. They were sick babies that required more attention than our twenty-three week old so they required a longer stay. Even after all of this as a mom I cried like a baby seeing a cannula in my child's nose morning until night at home. You begin to ask yourself why me? Well I don't have the answer to that and probably never will I'm just grateful to God our son made it out alive.

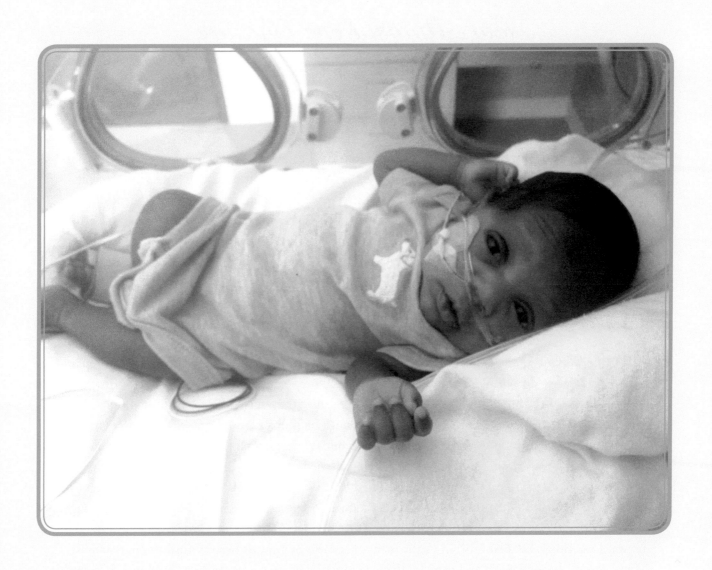

6

New Atmosphere Change

Now faith is the assurance of things hoped for, the conviction of things not seen. Hebrews 11:1 ESV

After arriving to Giovanni's temporary home from the hospital he was acting weird because the atmosphere changed. He was no longer inside the Whale room in his incubator so we knew it was going to be a challenge for all of us. God had took us on a long three month journey but we still had work to do with our son. I was a bit nervous the previous night before we took him home trying to ensure everything was perfect for his arrival. Giovanni was not only my first child but he tested our strength and how much trust we actually had in God. I wanted nothing but the best for our child as a mom never accepting any sickness that may come upon him. Since day one our eyes was only fixed on God and as you can see he was there until the very end. When God says I will never leave you or forsaken you trust me he stands on his word.

Meanwhile, when night fell that's when the complications came in and I wasn't sure I was prepared for it. My advice to all NICU parents is to immediately start teaching your baby how to distinguish night from day. It can be more challenging for us because they actually would sleep all day/night in the NICU. If they were born full term they would be more exposed to more sun light and it wouldn't take them as long from experience. After you have overcome this stage all else will fall into place. As for Giovanni since all babies are different I tried my best to keep him up during the day with noise. Also, minimum sun exposure helped him as well and this made him have a peaceful sleep at night. It did take three weeks but that's great compared to most. However, the advantage NICU babies have over full term babies is they are mainly independent in my own opinion. The reason I say this is because a NICU baby is in an isolette by him or herself until the parents visit. Many parents have to work and can't be there as much. The nurses sometimes hold but they can't all the time if there is more than one baby to tend to. A baby that's full term leaves the mother's womb and gets to go home with her. So there is a big difference between them. I can say Giovanni gained so much independence by growing outside the womb. When he came home he immediately started sleeping by himself in his own bed which was great for us. We didn't fear SIDS because Giovanni was on equipment and God was in control. If something happened we already knew it would have been a part of God's will and we wouldn't have questioned him. When God bring your child this far you can rest assured that he has a purpose for him. We had to attend classes before our child was allowed to come home with us. I thought this was a little crazy honestly because they have people that meet the criteria and their baby still is not getting the best treatment at home. As we gained more knowledge on how to care for a small baby we began to appreciate the extra training. CPR is always nice to know because anyone can need it at anytime not just babies.

Sleeping in the same room as your baby can be really comforting to them because they have been in the NICU so long. On the other hand, they may be independent but it's very important your love is shown at all times. Both parents should still give hand hugs even at home because it makes your little one feel safe in the atmosphere. You have to remember that your baby knows the scent of your body so this in another factor that's important when getting your baby to transition to their home. Me personally I prefer to sleep in arms reach of my baby because if he needs me I'm nearby. A monitor is fine but having an actual set of eyes on your baby is always the better choice. Always remember to do what's best for your miracle. You could never be too careful!

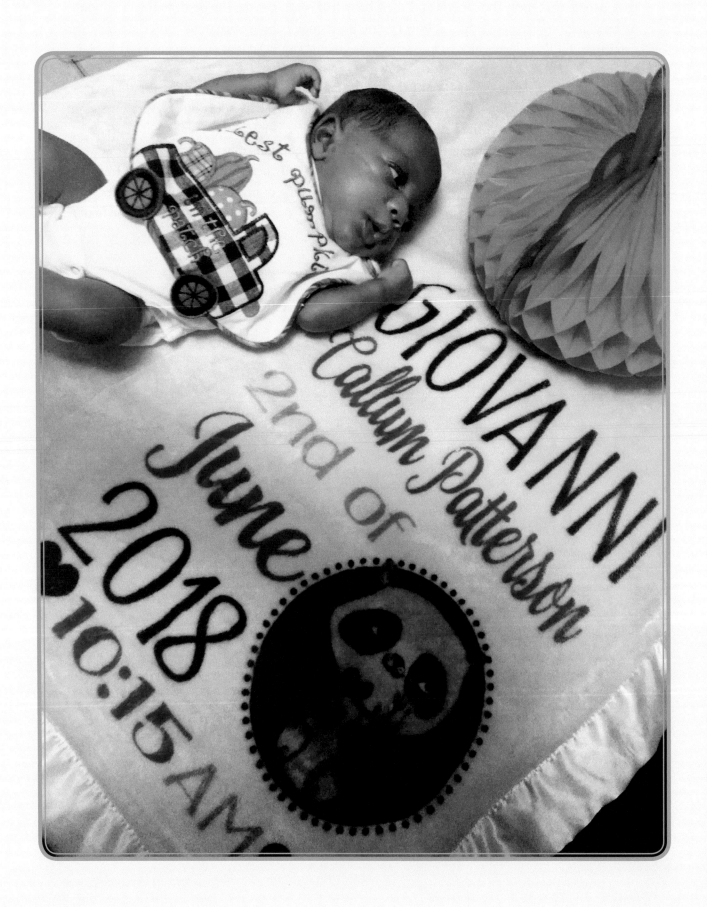

7
CHAPTER

Walking in Faith

And whatever you ask in prayer, you will receive, if you have faith.

Matthew 21:22 ESV

In November Giovanni was only home for a month and a half. One day I prayed to God and stopped using the oxygen equipment. I was scared to take him off not knowing the outcome but I knew God wanted me to set my son free. God gave me the strength to do this because I would have been held accountable. God saw otherwise and everything worked out for the better. In spite of that same day I was thinking silently to myself (keep in mind Giovanni is almost five months at this time) why would God spare our child's life if he would let his life go without oxygen. God is so powerful he was able to work through the mind of man using technology to keep our one pound three ounce son here. I will continue to give God the glory. I don't know what Giovanni's purpose is that God wants him to fulfill but I can expect it to be great. As his parent's we will continue to encourage him by the grace of God ensuring that Giovanni continue to live for God. Furthermore, people may not understand that we prayed and fasted for our child several months. We didn't just want a child we wanted a child that we can raise and give back to God. Anyone can produce a child but it's much better when you can raise he or she to live for God. We aren't perfect but we will try our best to keep that promise to God. If you haven't dealt with a child on oxygen before it can be pretty challenging. I didn't randomly take Giovanni off of oxygen due to my own selfishness but I just trusted God more. I didn't see that it was needed for a whole year as recommended by the doctor. I refuse to accept any sickness dealing with my child's life. Just know God is still the same God no matter what the situation may be. Never handicap your baby for anyone! All babies are different for example, some babies need oxygen born at thirty-five weeks. Our faith may lie in two different places but if your reading this book I'm praying for your strength. Just remember our son Giovanni was born on June 2, 2018 but his original due date was September 29, 2018. He came out three months early coming home three weeks before his due date (which even his doctor couldn't figure it out) on 0.1% oxygen he was supposed to have for I believe a year. Giovanni got taken off oxygen at home only a month and a half of being home. Now you tell me if God can't do anything. He's amazing and he done so many wonders for our son right before our eyes it's too good not to share. Keep in mind when I told the oxygen doctor I took him off he was a little that Giovanni couldn't handle it on his own. So he made a immediate appointment to test if the oxygen was needed. The whole entire visit my nerves were a little wrecked because I thought Giovanni would make me out a liar. Well apparently I was wrong because the doctor came back and said I will write him off this is you guys last time seeing me. This was such a relief knowing that I made one of the best decisions for my child I could ever make. My heart was rejoicing being that the doctor use his own oxygen at the office and approved my child to be off. What a great feeling as a parent! I immediately contacted Calvin and jetted out of the office so fast. I was speeding so fast I thought I left my Sketchers behind. Apart from this my advice to you as parents two people praying is better than one. As long as you can pray consider it done because God can do the same thing for you as he done for us! We tend to sometimes get distracted by those around us who haven't even been through the half of it fix your eyes and ears on Jesus. Blot out all the white noise from doctors, family, co-workers, etc. and exercise your faith by praying. God has done miraculous things for us and I can't help but to be excited. Every journey isn't easy because we had some rough spots. We learned that the only way we can overcome our obstacles is through praying and fasting.

8
CHAPTER

Claim No Diagnosed Illness

I am the Lord who heals you. Exodus 15:26 AMP

So this get pretty interesting and funny due to doctors believing they hold all the power of illnesses. First and foremost no one ever had a thyroid problem on my side of the family. Calvin also mentioned not to his knowledge anyone on his side either. So when Giovanni left the hospital they told me he had to be on thyroid medication (one tablet a day) for three years. Being that it doesn't run in the family was a tad bit confusing why would they say something is wrong with his thyroid. A thyroid is a butterfly-shaped gland that sits low on the front of the neck. I refuse to give my child medication that can possibly cause other issues for three years. I continued to go to the visits for thyroid and every time we went they would check Giovanni's levels. The doctor would call me and say the levels were normal she can see the medicine is doing great. Every visit I would ask her is it a possibility that Giovanni can stop taking the medicine before three years and she said no. So keep in mind we kept going for maybe five months and she kept saying the same answer. Therefore, one day I could no longer hold my secret in pretending everything was okay when it wasn't. I asked her for the last time is it possible he can be taken off the medicine since his levels are always great after blood work she replied, no he needs it. Finally, I tell her my secret Giovanni only took the medicine twice literally since we left the hospital. Her mouth opened so wide a fly could have flew in it and had a home. She was like so why haven't you been giving him his medication? I replied, I don't trust medication but I do trust Jesus. Furthermore, no one on either side of his family suffer from thyroid disease. The whole time I had been going to the doctor for five consistent months just for the fun of it. Giovanni was healed and delivered from all things the day he stepped foot out the hospital so we didn't accept any of it. I don't expect them to understand that because it's a spiritual thing and God was presenting his marvelous works right before our eyes. So the moral of this is even though you are diagnosed with an illness never claim it or rejoice in it. When God heals he want us to appreciate it and continue to worship him in spirit and in truth.

9
CHAPTER

True Repentance

"Repent, then, and turn to God, so that your sins may be wiped out, that
times of refreshing may come from the Lord." Acts 3:19 NIV

Sometimes believe it or not we may do things in life that's not right to ourselves and others. We
probably ask for forgiveness but still hold the foolishness in our hearts. We should genuinely repent
(turn away from) for the remissions of our sins and fix our heart on the things of Christ. If not
then what we do to others can impact the close people around you. For example, that's why we
have to deny ourselves and repent daily. Satan has his way of making us comfortable in our sins.
That's why when sickness or whatever else comes upon us we find it hard to battle it because we
are already so comfortable in our sins, instead we just embrace it. I'm definitely here to tell you
don't let sin or any illness overtake you. Our son wasn't just healed by faith we had to honest with
God and repent then he moved on our situation. We as parents are responsible for what happens
with our children but are sometimes in denial. Children can't pray for themselves so we hold the
responsibility as parents to pray for them. I don't care how busy you are make sure your depositing
not just money in the bank but your prayers as well. God is the real banker and when he see the
prayers being deposited consistently he will move on your child's situation. It's not easy trust me
when we are living in a world that's very entertaining and want to be above God. All I know is God
made me a believer even more when he made my son completely well. Giovanni could have died
and he probably would have if we responded selfishly. Instead we utilized the greatest gift of all
prayer to the one that gives life and takes it. We prayed for months at a time and God never waivered
because he knew we would strive to live for him from that day forward. We made a promise to God
that if he let our baby live we would raise him and give him back to him. I don't know what God
has in store for Giovanni but I do know he is blessed abundantly with life itself. However, if your
child is young or old please instill the word of God in them so they may never depart from it.

10
CHAPTER

Loving Visible & Appreciating Invisible

So we fix our eyes not on what is seen, but on what is unseen, since what is seen
is temporary, but what is unseen is eternal. 2 Corinthians 4:18 NIV

Sometimes children can have visible illnesses that we aren't so happy with because we can physically see it. Illnesses such as Down Syndrome, Mental health issues, Birth Defects, etc. no one want to see their child with a disfigured appearance. When we put our trust in God only, we don't have to accept the physical appearance we aren't pleased with. He is working it out invisibly which is the things we don't see. It's so easy to accept it because we sometimes feel there is no way out. If God showed us everything, he will give us before we pray to him, we would only do it under that circumstance. He wants you to love what you can see and love what you can't see as well. God doesn't make any mistakes and he does everything for a reason. Appreciate him and cast all your worries on him the invisible is way better than the visible because it's eternal. I rather my child have eternal life over anything. As parents we imagine delivering perfect babies but sometimes God has other plans. Learn to appreciate everything being grateful and he will move on your child situation. Don't be ashamed or anything because no child is the same. When I saw Giovanni looking like a 1lb. 3o.z. alien trust me I was a little disappointed considering we had done everything right to our knowledge. I was in awe because I made plans for a baby that wasn't even here yet. I couldn't do half the things with Giovanni that you could do with a full term baby. Now my son is hearty and healthy enjoying every moment of life. I had to learn personally to not judge his outer appearance and trust in the unseen which is God that worked it all out. From experience try not to lean into your own understanding and stand on the word of God. There will be days that things seem cloudy and you lose hope just remember prayer can change any circumstance. It's never good to judge the outer appearance because for any baby to withstand all the treatment they are true warriors.

11
CHAPTER

Creating Bond

But the fruit of the spirit is love, joy, peace, patience, kindness,
goodness, and faithfulness. Galatians 5:22 AMP

When people see the word bond they immediately think about an attachment with someone, but whoever looks at it like a bond with God? A bond with God is more precious than any bond you can ever encounter because it creates a stronger bond with your child. Before I got baptized in Jesus name I honestly didn't know how to properly bond with Giovanni being that he was born with a disability three months early. I had to seek God more which I'm still continuing to do so in order to have patience with my child. It can become a little frustrating when you feel like your baby is lacking on some things he should be doing when you see other babies do them exceptionally well. Other moms have came up to me at doctor visits saying, "he's fairly small". I would reply, yes he was born three months early. Three months early was literally a part of our language everywhere we went. When you can create a solid bond with Jesus first you will be able to conquer all these things. Think about it if you see other moms getting out the car perfectly fine with their children and your taking twenty minutes with just one child, equipment, etc. How would you feel? You can't tell me that some part of you wouldn't want to give up. Well you can't give up and you need to tell yourself that in the end love, peace, joy and goodness will come out of the situation just keep being faithful to God. Talk to him when your driving, cooking, or doing any other hobby and create that bond that will bring you peace. I know if we got through it you can as well. Giovanni when you get old enough to read this yourself just know mommy had some tough times understanding, learning and appreciating the situation with the circumstances. Now I can say that God has instilled in me more love, patience and everything I need to ensure we give you back to him.

12
CHAPTER

Super Dad

He who spares accountability hates his son, but he who loves him
is careful to discipline him. Proverbs 13:24 NIV

I want to personally thank you Calvin for being the best father you could be to Giovanni. He's extremely blessed to have you, the wisdom of God, knowledge and truth you instill in him is amazing. I know he appreciates it and will never depart from it as long as God continue to allow you to be a super dad! Daddy thank you for being there for me and loving me always. You never gave up on me even when things got rough you just continued to pray me through. I enjoy and appreciate every moment spent with you at the hospital for three exhausting months. You would always visit with me every Tuesday even being hooked up to every existing wire, I will never forget the love you have shown during my roughest stages. Daddy I can say my spiritual father blessed me with an awesome earthly father and I wouldn't trade you for anything. Thank you for everything and I will always be grateful for you. -Giovanni Patterson & Mom

13
CHAPTER

The Walking Experience

For we walk by faith not by sight. 2 Corinthians 5:7 NIV

Mom's often ask me at what age did Giovanni walk since he was born three months early? To answer that question actually he walked at one years old and six months. Which is pretty discouraging because every time he would go for a check-up I would ask why. What I didn't understand was his outer appearance wasn't as strong for example, his legs looked strong but was weak. He honestly had an issue with balance and he couldn't keep it for thirty seconds. His dad and I began working with him more then one day he finally started walking on his own. To say he was so little his faith was strong because despite him falling every time Giovanni never gave up. Try teacher a baby that's already so independent how to walk it's frustrating. He or she will be looking forward to the day they don't need you anymore. In my mind I was looking at the appearance but the whole time Giovanni had more faith than we actually thought being he didn't walk by sight. When he did learn how to walk he was unstoppable but of course the falling continued. I'm telling you from experience it gets harder as the stages climb but with God all things are possible. You won't know unless you go through it that's why it's better to communicate with others rather than judge because you never know what their battle is. Giovanni encouraged me plenty of days I wanted to give up because he couldn't walk yet. I would always overlook the circumstance and immediately think I'm failing him as a mom. When he would fall he'd get up and smile like mom we got this and that's all I needed to pick myself back up. Every baby isn't the same but I can tell you if they are born a micro preemie it will be quite similar.

14
CHAPTER

Existing Inner Strength

May you be strengthened with all power, according to his glorious might,
for all endurance and patience with joy. Colossians 1:11 RSV

Situations may arise in our lives that we absolutely have no control over, but we get through them not knowing how. The reason is because God supplies us with inner strength but we typically doubt our capabilities that lies within us. We should have strength even when we are in our darkest moments in life. Giovanni put us in a dark place but we had to reach beyond that darkness using the inner strength that God supplied us with to get past it. It's interesting how people will speak negative things toward you and they have no idea that you are already weak. Instead they should be praying for your strength not backbiting. If you can't add to a person's situation in a positive manner then subtract your negative energy. We will never understand the ways of God, not even scientist can. It's very exhausting when you are weak and feel as though all hope is gone. You have many opinions for example, "your too old to have a child" but don't let that weaken your inner strength. In addition to this the devil will try to use people to destroy you or stress you out due to their own misery, simply ignore focusing only on Jesus. Keep in mind God will always have a reward for the wicked. On the other hand, if God didn't want you to have a child trust me he would have taken it. Continue telling yourself I'm strong and I will get through this. So don't pay attention to workers of iniquity just reach down and exhaust your inner strength through prayer. Make all your request be known to God not people because they can interfere with your strength especially if you aren't praying.

15
CHAPTER

Giovanni's Results

The Lord will guide you continually, watering your life when you are dry and keeping you healthy too. You will be like a well-watered garden, like an ever-flowing spring.

Isaiah 58:11 NLT

Giovanni was like a plant that needed to be watered in order to grow healthy. If you are a plant lover like myself then you definitely know what happens to a plant without water, it dies. Think about the time you grew your first plant, I'm pretty sure you were excited to see the results daily. It may have taken six weeks to grown but everyday you nourished that same plant awaiting the ending results. Furthermore, I say this because by Giovanni being my first child I had to continue watering his situation with the word of God in order for him to grow. In spite of his scar on his left hand he is a true warrior. I know he was in a lot of pain but God has so much mercy even in our sins, he saved him. The plant grew into a beautiful toddler but we had to water it daily. Now our son is blessed not only with life itself but opportunities.

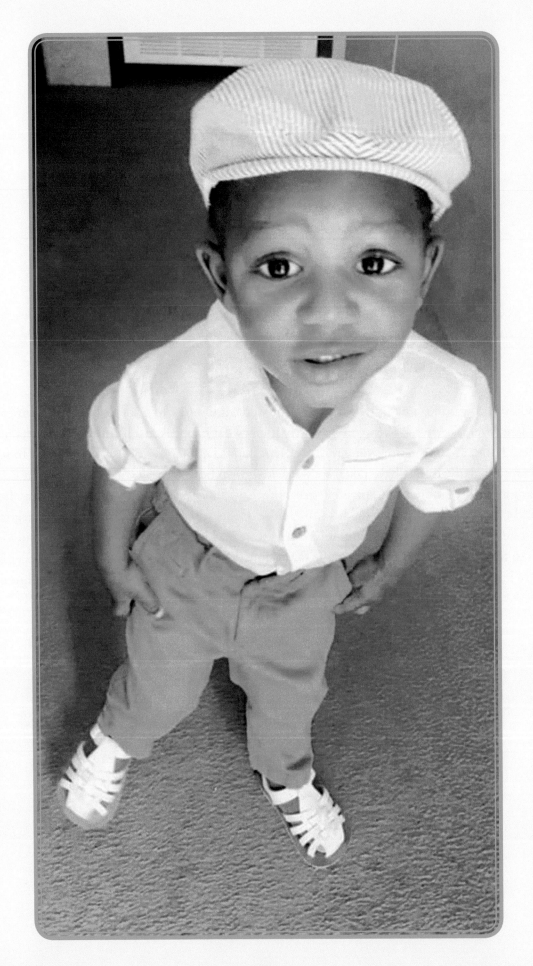

16
CHAPTER

Ending Encouragement

Therefore encourage one another and build each other up, just as
in fact you are doing. 1 Thessalonians 5:11 NIV

We are happy to encourage anyone as a parent of a miracle that you will
get through it just as we did. We would like to provide you with some
great scriptures that you can read when your in that dark place.

1. Lamentations 3:22 NIV
2. Jeremiah 29:11 NIV
3. Psalm 94:18-19 NIV
4. Psalm 46:1-3 NIV
5. Thessalonians 5:16-18 NIV
6. Psalm 34:18 NIV

17
CHAPTER

Giovanni Callum Patterson

Listen my son to your father's instruction and do not forsake your mother's teaching.
They are a garland to grace your head and a chain to adorn your neck. Proverbs1:8-9

Dear Giovanni, we have written this book to reveal your story to anyone we can encourage.
You are a blessing within itself. We are so excited to be your parents and we want you to know
that God gets all the glory. I pray you never depart from the word of God because it's instilled
inside of you. Always be true to yourself remaining humble at all times. Circumstances
may arise in your life but as long as God allow us to be here we will be. I refer to you as my
challenging child because you definitely put our faith to the test. Let me tell you a little
secret some nights mom would get in the car get half way to the hospital and turn around. I
had so many tears in my eyes being afraid of the phone call I would receive from the doctor
or nurse. However, for some odd reason they would always call us with bad news at night
time and we didn't understand. So I started coming to the hospital really late when your dad
went to work so I could receive the news in person. We made many sacrifices for you that
you will never understand because we love you so much. It honestly disturbed me when I saw
some parents visiting very little it only motivated me to visit twice as much. I was so excited
when they finally allowed me to assist with baths. Your nurse was very sweet at night and
she always looked forward to me coming. The night she told me I was able to brush your
hair for the first time meant everything to me. If I wouldn't visit three times a day I would
definitely be there twice a day. The first part of the day I would read you your first Bible
collection that your dad bought from the gift shop at the hospital. Our second visit would
consist of hand hugs which I was afraid of due to the texture of your gel-like skin. We really
are grateful for this experience being that you are here today. Some babies at the time you
were in the hospital didn't make it and I prayed with their parents. It could have been the
other way around but God has plans for you. Your dad and I also made a promise that if
he let you live we would raise you up to give back to him the right way. Further more, you
are an amazing son and big brother to baby Salathiel. He will grow up healthy and strong
remembering every moment you spent with him. I find it intriguing how your two years
old now cleaning your own room. You are a very responsible little guy, don't ever change for
anyone. We appreciate you taking the time to learn how important it is to be potty trained
before the age of two. I actually started potty training you at eighteen months and you only

made four accidents I'm aware of. You have made us so proud within these two years Giovanni because you never gave up. No matter how much you were pushed to the limit you mastered everything that came your way. We meant that we wouldn't allow your situation to become you and we didn't. You are strong, loving, sweet, smart, caring, and independent child of God. We look forward to seeing what the future has in store for you and we love you!

-Mom & Dad

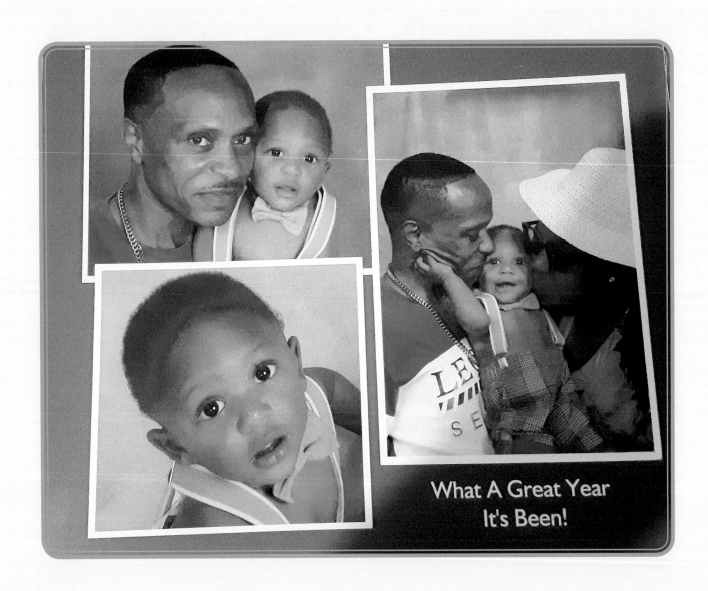

What A Great Year
It's Been!

Gallery

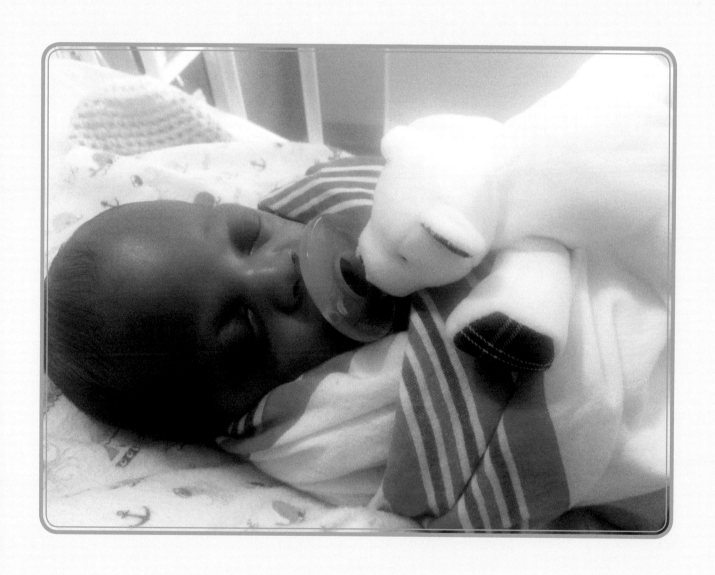

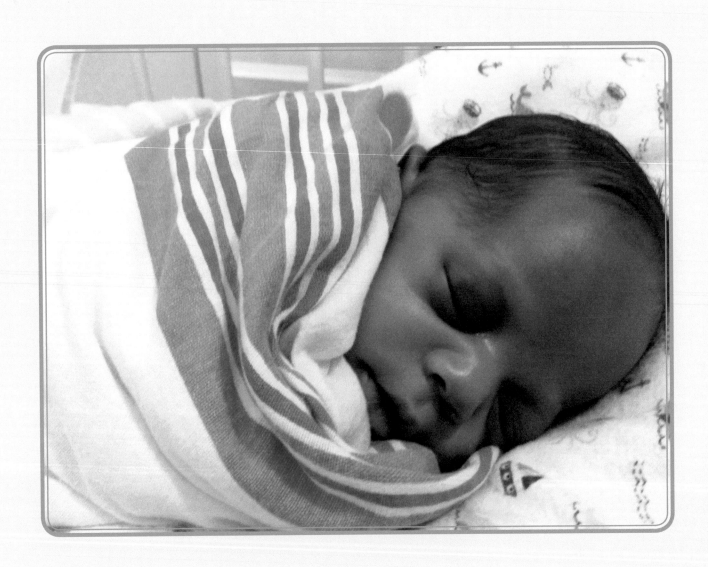

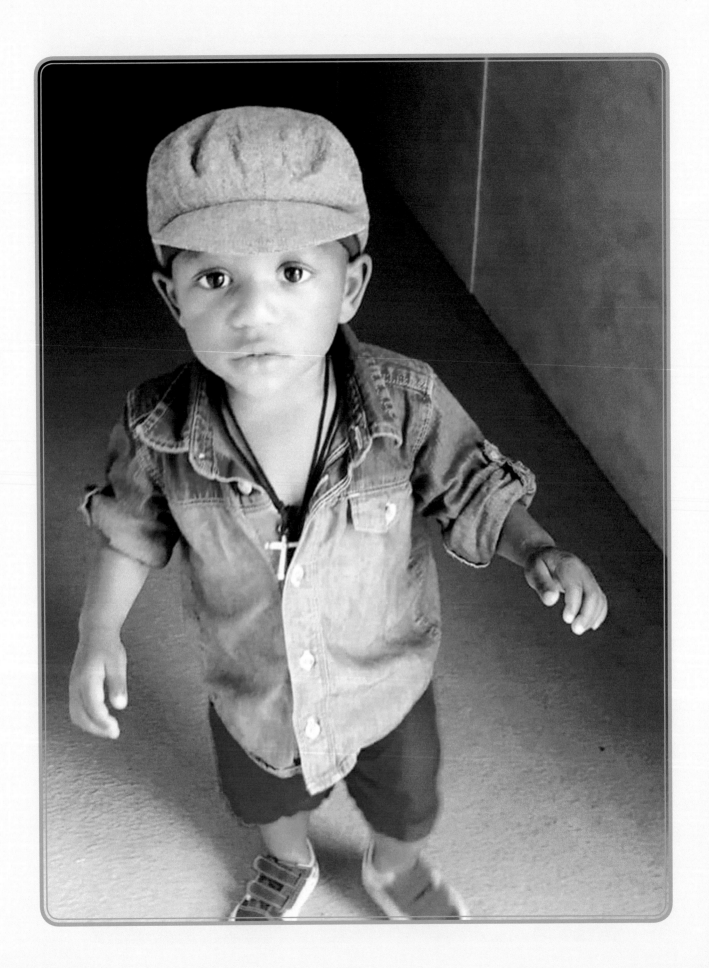

Printed in the United States
By Bookmasters